CABINS
THE NEW STYLE

CABINS
THE NEW STYLE

JAMES GRAYSON TRULOVE

COLLINS|DESIGN
An Imprint of HarperCollinsPublishers

FIRST EDITION

FIRST PUBLISHED IN 2006 BY
COLLINS DESIGN
AN IMPRINT OF HARPER COLLINS*PUBLISHERS*
10 EAST 53RD STREET
NEW YORK, NY 10022
TEL: (212) 207-7000
FAX: (212) 207-7654
COLLINSDESIGN@HARPERCOLLINS.COM
WWW.HARPERCOLLINS.COM

DISTRIBUTED THROUGHOUT THE WORLD BY:
HARPER COLLINS*PUBLISHERS*
10 EAST 53RD STREET
NEW YORK, NY 10022
FAX: (212) 207-7654

PACKAGED BY:
GRAYSON PUBLISHING, LLC
JAMES G. TRULOVE, PUBLISHER
1250 28TH STREET NW
WASHINGTON, DC 20007
(202) 337-1380
jtrulove@aol.com

DESIGN DIRECTIONS BY:
AGNIESZKA STACHOWICZ
ag_stach@yahoo.com

LIBRARY OF CONGRESS CATALOGING-IN-PUBLICATION DATA

TRULOVE, JAMES GRAYSON.
  CABINS : THE NEW STYLE / JAMES GRAYSON TRULOVE.-- 1ST ED.
    P. CM.
  ISBN-13: 978-0-06-089349-1 (HARDCOVER)
  ISBN-10: 0-06-089349-4 (HARDCOVER)
  1. VACATION HOMES--UNITED STATES. 2. INTERIOR DECORATION--UNITED
STATES--HISTORY--21ST CENTURY. I. TITLE.
  NK2195.V34T78 2006
  728.7'30973--DC22

                        2005034920

MANUFACTURED IN CHINA
FIRST PRINTING, 2006
1 2 3 4 5 6 7 8 9 / 06 05 04 03

CONTENTS

9   FOREWORD

10   EDELWEISS CABIN

22   ANDERSON CABIN

32   CATARACT RANCH

44   WHEATSHEAF RESIDENCE

56   BLUFF RESIDENCE

66   BOYD RESIDENCE

78   METROPOLITAN CABIN

90   GOLOB-FREEMAN CABIN

100   CARSON CABIN

114   EVANS RESIDENCE

128   MEADOW CABIN

142   MATTHEW CABIN

154   WINTERGREEN CABIN

166   VINEYARD CABIN

176   CANYON CABIN

FOREWORD

Tell friends you own a cabin and the image of a quaint, one-room log dwelling in the woods—think Abe Lincoln—probably pops into their heads. An outhouse, no electricity, and a wood-burning cookstove completes the image.

Well, welcome to the twenty-first century. In *Cabins: The New Style*, fifteen projects have been chosen to illustrate the incredible range of styles, finishes, and sizes that make up the modern cabin. Wood is still a primary building material, and yes, logs are also used sometimes, but lots of glass, recycled materials, and low-maintenance metals are now star players. On the design front, most architects are particularly sensitive to the need to make the cabin seem at home within its natural surroundings and not dominate the site on which it is located. To this end, careful attention is paid to the exterior color palette, to the massing of the buildings, and most important, to the preservation of as much existing vegetation as possible.

Inside, all the cabins chosen for this book seem to have one thing in common: an interior that is warm and inviting and that offers a secure sanctuary from the wilderness at the doorstep. Which is not to say that nature is excluded. To the contrary, big porches and extravagant expanses of windows and sliding doors encourage eye-to-eye contact with passing creatures of the forest.

For our forebears, the cabin was a symbol of humble beginnings. Today, the cabin offers its owners an opportunity to escape from a far more complex life and return, however briefly, to peaceful, natural surroundings—but with style!

LEFT: *Meadow Cabin, Balance Associates; photography by Steve Keating*
RIGHT: *Vineyard Cabin, Moskow Architects; photography by Eric Roth*

EDELWEISS CABIN

ARCHITECT BALANCE ASSOCIATES ARCHITECTS
LOCATION WASHINGTON

This 1,600 square-foot cabin is perched on the edge of a hillside above a valley in eastern Washington. The prime building location was a narrow strip on the edge of the hill, which inspired the cabin's elongated floor plan that allows all of the rooms to have spectacular views of the river, valley, and surrounding mountains. The main living area has a large window wall that faces south to capture the heat from the sun as well as the view. Sliding glass doors open onto a generous deck, where an outdoor shower is located that connects directly to the main bathroom. The deck pops out and the guardrail wraps around the shower to provide privacy while still allowing sweeping views of the valley floor below.

An open stair connects the master bedroom suite to the living room. A small den outside the master bedroom overlooks the living room. The kitchen is tucked near the entry, opening out to the living room. A guest bedroom, children's bedroom, laundry, and bath are located below the master suite.

PHOTOGRAPHER PETER BASTIANELLI-KERZE

UPPER FLOOR PLAN

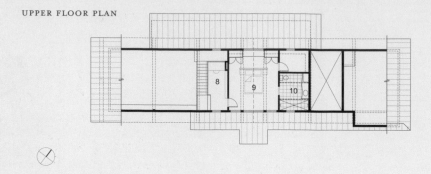

PREVIOUS PAGES: *Sliding glass doors open to a generous deck. Clear-stained cedar board-and-batten siding reflects the rural character of the ranch and farm buildings in the surrounding area. Red-painted rough-sawn plywood siding is used for accents. A garage is separated from the main cabin by a breezeway.* RIGHT: *The cabin is perched at the edge of a hill overlooking the valley and mountains.*

MAIN FLOOR PLAN

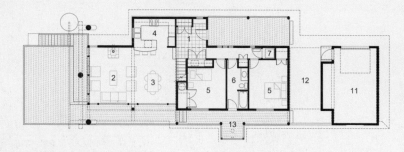

1 entry
2 living
3 dining
4 kitchen
5 bedroom
6 bath
7 laundry
8 den
9 master bedroom
10 master bath
11 garage
12 breezeway
13 outdoor shower

SITE PLAN

SECTIONS

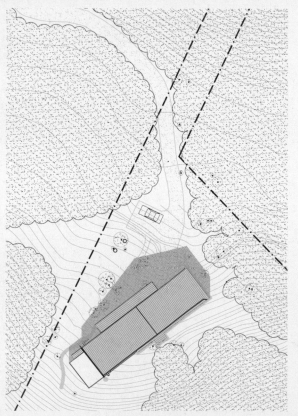

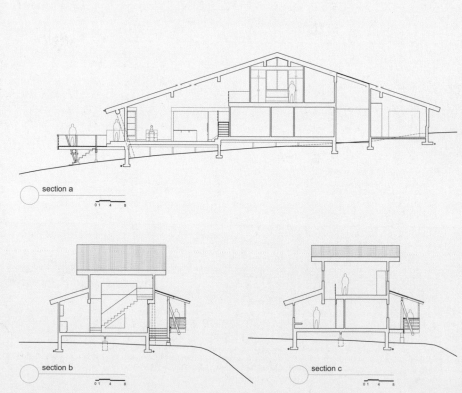

section a

0 1   4   8

section b

0 1   4   8

section c

0 1   4   8

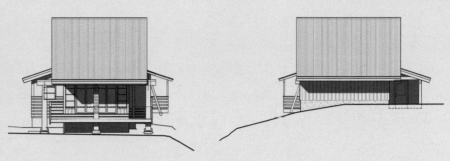

NORTH ELEVATION

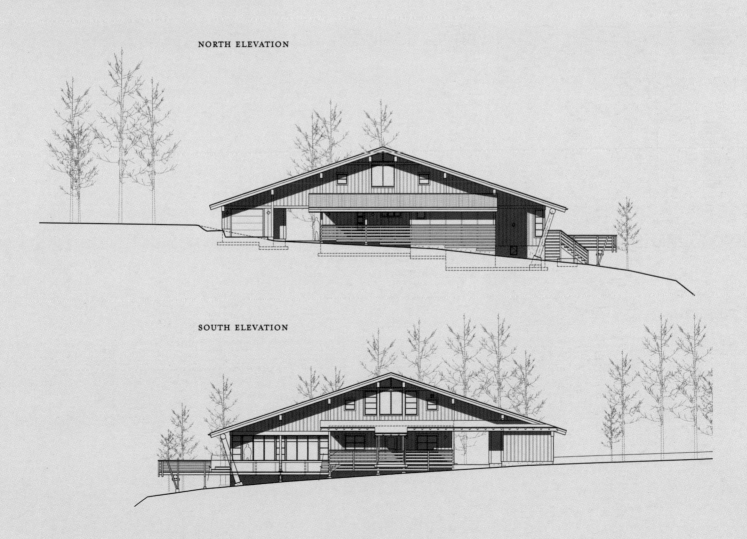

SOUTH ELEVATION

EDELWEISS CABIN

13

ABOVE LEFT: *A sketch of the cabin shows the garage separated from the dwelling by a breezeway.*
LEFT, ABOVE, AND RIGHT: *The deck cantilevers over the site, providing a viewing platform and an area for entertaining.*

LEFT AND ABOVE: *The ceiling
in the two-story living room is
rough-sawn plywood with one-by-
three-inch wood battens.*

LEFT: *The master bedroom suite is located on the second floor, accessed via an open stair. A small, open den is located at the top of the stairs.*
ABOVE: *The master bedroom is tucked under the eaves of the house.*

RIGHT: *Polycarbonate glazing panels are used for the shower partition in the master bathroom.*
FOLLOWING PAGES: *The post-and-beam construction consists of Douglas fir log columns and glu-laminate beams.*

ANDERSON CABIN

ARCHITECT **DAVID SALMELA**

LOCATION **WISCONSIN**

Although recently completed, this 18-foot-wide Wisconsin cabin conveys a sense of history and timelessness with its steep metal roofs and lap wood siding. The three-story white clapboard structure has two rooms on each floor, separated by a stairway and bathroom core. An old-fashioned porch is attached to the rear. The cabin is located in a historic district in a small Wisconsin town on the edge of the Chequamegon Bay, which projects into Lake Superior.

Certain design features lend a grandeur to the the home, despite its modest façade. Broad, exterior stairs lead ceremoniously to the entrance. Inside, oversized windows create an openness that intensifies the amount of interior light and creates strong visual connections with the landscape. The Alvar Aalto furniture adds to the overall minimalist and modernist quality of the project while respecting the many historical references incorporated into the cabin's design.

PHOTOGRAPHER **PETER BASTIANELLI-KERZE**

PREVIOUS PAGES: *Oversized
windows lend a grandeur to the
18-foot-wide cabin.*
RIGHT: *Decks and porches
extend the living space during
summer months.*

BASEMENT PLAN   FIRST FLOOR PLAN   UPPER FLOOR PLAN

0'   10'

ELEVATIONS   SITE PLAN

SECTION

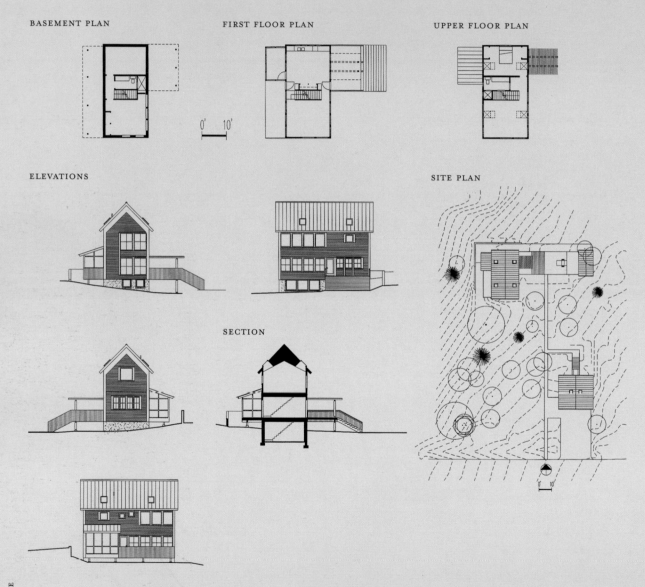

ABOVE AND RIGHT: *The small house sits at the top of a broad, inviting entry staircase.*

LEFT AND ABOVE: *A classic exterior gives way to a decidedly modern interior complete with minimalist Aalto furnishings.* FOLLOWING PAGES: *The light, open kitchen has a decidedly country feel to it.*

CATARACT RANCH

ARCHITECT SEMPLE BROWN DESIGN

LOCATION COLORADO

The design of this single-family 3,000-square-foot residence on 36 acres in Colorado responds directly to its natural surroundings and to the panoramic views of aspens, meadows, and mountains. The house was sited to nestle against a large forest of aspens, with the main room seemingly floating on a sea of sagebrush, taking advantage of the contrasting views of ranch-land meadows and the dramatic Gore Range.

The exterior consists of a carefully chosen palette of materials and colors that correspond to agricultural buildings indigenous to the area and natural surroundings. Materials include deeply grooved corrugated metal panels, lead-coated copper, and straight-grain Douglas fir soffits. The interior is clad primarily in a horizontal tongue-and-groove wood that provides texture and warmth.

Bedrooms are stacked in a two-story wing separate from the large, single-story wing that houses the living, dining, and kitchen areas in an open plan. In this area, full-height doors and expanses of glass make good use of passive ventilation, solar heat, and broad views.

PHOTOGRAPHER RON POLLAND

BASEMENT

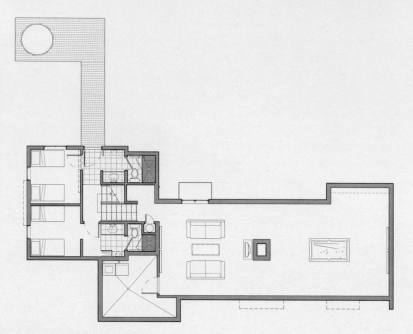

SITE PLAN

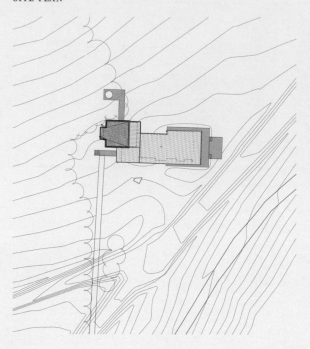

MAIN LEVEL

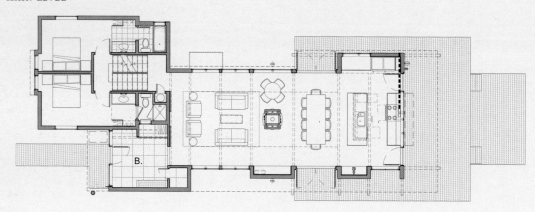

B.

PREVIOUS PAGES: *The exterior color and material pallete was chosen to blend the cabin with its natural surroundings.*

UPPER LEVEL

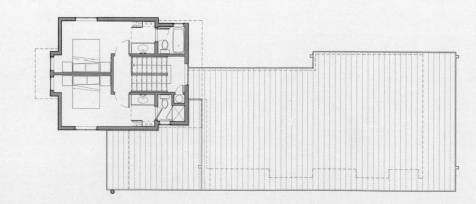

WEST ELEVATION

EAST ELEVATION

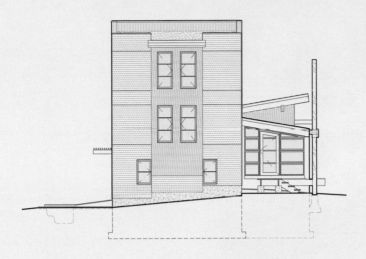

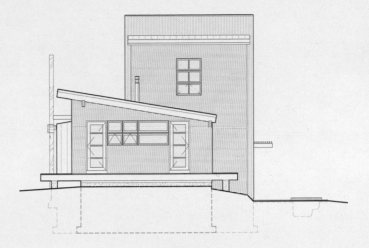

NORTH ELEVATION

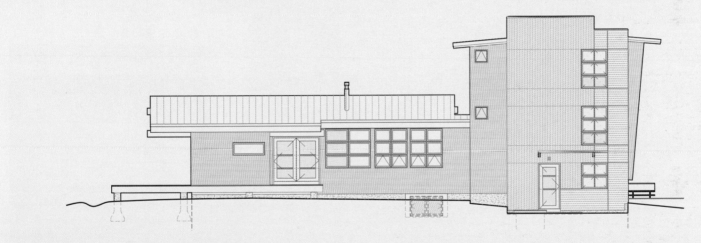

LONGITUDINAL SECTION

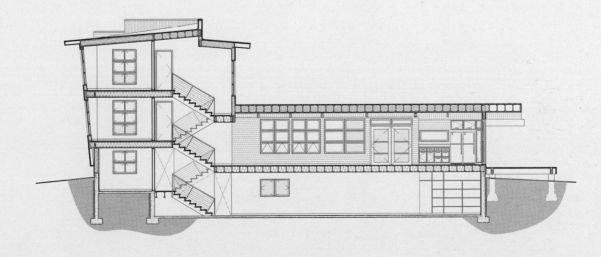

LEFT: *The sleeping quarters are housed in the enclosed two-story wing.*
ABOVE: *Public areas are contained in the one-story part of the house.*

LEFT AND RIGHT: *Horizontal tongue–and–groove cedar creates a warm and inviting interior, as seen here in the living and dining area.*

LEFT AND ABOVE: *The kitchen and dining areas*
RIGHT: *Bedrooms located in the two-story wing are cozier and have smaller windows.*

WHEATSHEAF RESIDENCE

ARCHITECT JESSE JUDD ARCHITECTS
LOCATION MELBOURNE, AUSTRALIA

Wood is the building material that first comes to mind when one thinks of cabins, but this simple yet dramatic cabin that appears to float above the wooded landscape has an outer skin made entirely of steel.

Located a couple of hours from Melbourne, Australia, in an area known for its lakes and spas, this cabin appears as a gentle fold of corrugated steel where the floor becomes the back wall and then the roof. A surrounding deck made from recycled rough-sawn wood has been kept low so that no balustrade is required. An adjacent, connected linear structure contains three bedrooms that are accessed via a glass-walled passageway. The entry is marked by a magenta wall that is parallel to the bedroom wing.

This entry leads to the main living area contained within the folded plane. The curved wall, ceiling, and floor are veneered in blood-red stained hoop pine plywood. It is a cozy but loft-like space that completely enfolds the occupant. Extensive glazing surrounds this space, which emits a brilliant, warm glow when viewed from the outside in the evening.

PHOTOGRAPHER PETER BENNETTS

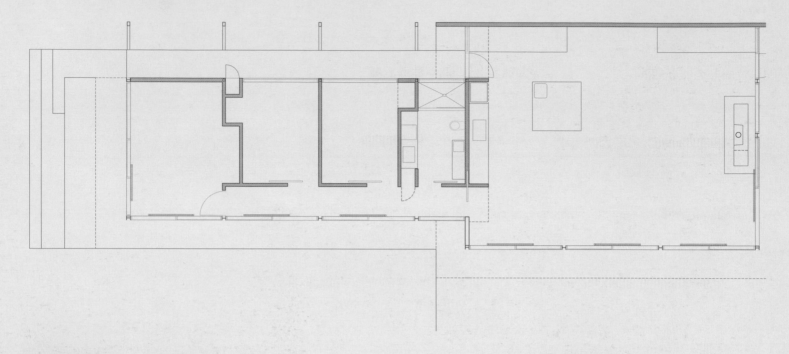

PREVIOUS PAGES, LEFT, AND RIGHT: *The cabin appears to hover above the rural landscape. The low deck becomes an extension of the ground plane. A fireplace anchors one end of the primary living space.*

ABOVE: *The deck was kept low so as to eliminate the need for guardrails.*
RIGHT: *The formal entrance is marked by a corrugated steel wall painted magenta.*

LEFT AND ABOVE: *The primary living space, consisting of the living, dining, and kitchen areas, is contained within a cocoon of plywood stained blood red.*

FAR LEFT: *The minimalist stainless steel kitchen*

LEFT: *The glass–walled corridor connecting the three bedrooms*

ABOVE: *Clerestory windows bring light into the bathroom.*

FOLLOWING PAGES: *A view at dusk from the bedroom wing to the primary living area*

BLUFF CABIN

ARCHITECT TURNBULL GRIFFIN & HAESLOOP

LOCATION NORTHERN CALIFORNIA

This vacation house is situated along the top of a bluff directly across from a stand of three cypress trees. There are houses close by on either side of the lot and design guidelines for this community mandate a 16-foot height limit. Therefore, the architect's challenge was to create a sense of privacy that uniquely captures the grand scale of the coastline directly in front of the site.

The result is a 2,300-square-foot, four-bedroom house and garage, which is divided by an outdoor spine, a courtyard that runs through the center of the house. This large, translucent covered space is the focus of the house, directing views to the trees and coastline directly ahead. An exterior stair leads to a small second-story deck over the entryway, which allows for better viewing of the rocky coastline that lies below.

The living room, dining room, and kitchen occupy the northern half of the house while the bedrooms are in the southern half. There is also a guest room, a fish-cleaning station, and an octagonal courtyard that greets the visitor at the entry to the house.

PHOTOGRAPHER JIM ALINDER

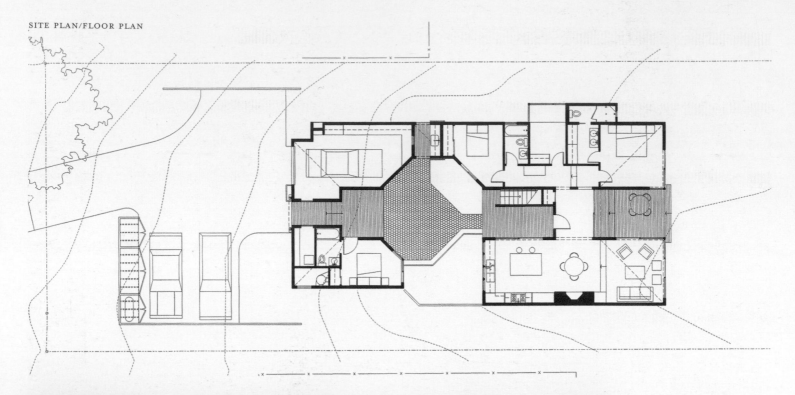

**PREVIOUS PAGES AND TOP
RIGHT:** *A view of the stairs leading
to the second floor observation deck
as seen from the octagonal courtyard*
LEFT: *A view past the octagonal
courtyard to the entry*
RIGHT: *A view of the ocean from
the central spine*

LEFT AND ABOVE: *The kitchen
and dining areas are positioned so that
they have sweeping views of the ocean.*

ABOVE: *The living room*
RIGHT: *Cedar is used for the*
bedroom corridor and most other
areas of the house.

BOYD RESIDENCE

ARCHITECT TURNBULL GRIFFIN & HAESLOOP
LOCATION NORTHERN CALIFORNIA

Located along a bluff over the Pacific Ocean north of San Francisco, this recently completed vacation house is actually four separate structures—the main house, two children's bedrooms, and a garage with a hot tub room—organized around a central courtyard that is protected from the wind. A glass-roofed arcade connects the three main buildings and helps frame the views through the house to the coastal landscape and the ocean beyond. The longest block fronts onto the ocean and contains the living, kitchen, dining, and great room in the center, flanked by support spaces, the master bedroom, and a study to either side.

The great room has large expanses of glass framed by bookcases that act as columns, providing a sense of enclosure while simultaneously bringing the views of the landscape and garden into and through the house. The two-bedroom cabins for the owner's sons are designed to double as guest rooms, one with a loft and small study, the other with a larger open room.

The house is constructed of wooden shingles with vertical-grain Douglas fir interiors. The ceiling is an exposed construction with trusses that rely on a tension rod in the center to give the roof a light and airy structure.

PHOTOGRAPHER JIM ALINDER

SITE PLAN

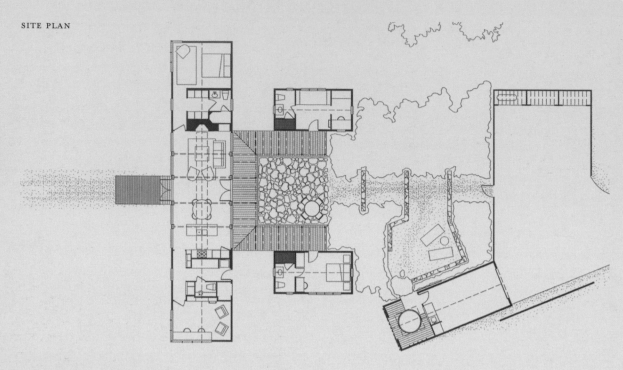

PREVIOUS PAGES: *A view of the ceiling in the great room, with exposed trusses*

RIGHT: *A view from the courtyard through the main house to the Pacific*

AXONOMETRIC

The courtyard is protected from the wind, and is flanked by guest bedrooms and the main house.

LEFT AND RIGHT: *The courtyard is protected from the wind, and is flanked by guest bedrooms and the main house.*

FOLLOWING PAGES: *Support columns containing bookcases are organized around the great room, with large windows overlooking the seacoast.*

LEFT: *A guest cabin with sleeping loft.*
ABOVE: *The hot tub room in the garage has a window overlooking the Pacific.*
FOLLOWING PAGES: *A view of the compound showing the main house, a guest cabin, and the garage with the hot tub room.*

METROPOLITAN CABIN

ARCHITECT BALANCE ASSOCIATES ARCHITECTS
LOCATION WASHINGTON

This 800-square-foot cabin is located along a river in eastern Washington. Its simple shape allowed for the use of structural insulated panels, which are fabricated off-site and delivered as a kit of parts, for efficient construction. The small cabin is organized around one central space, which functions as the living room, dining room, and kitchen. It is connected to the outside by a large, bright red window wall that opens onto a deck. The window frames two towering pine trees with a backdrop of nearby mountains. Two sleeping lofts are located on the second floor. They are connected by a small catwalk with one ladder access point to minimize the use of floor space below. The master bedroom is a nook off the living room that can be closed in with a large sliding door. A small bath is located off the side of the kitchen and bedroom nook.

The roof and lower-wall wainscot are sheathed in corrugated galvanized steel. The metal wainscot provides protection from the heavy snowfall the area receives. The main building is clad in rough-sawn cedar board-and-batten siding. The wooden windows are painted in a durable finish to reduce maintenance. The radiant-heated concrete floors are colored to match the decking, which expands the visual floor area of the cabin.

PHOTOGRAPHER STEVE KEATING

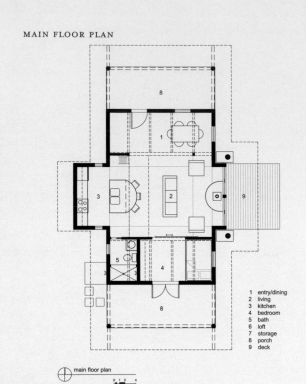

1 entry/dining
2 living
3 kitchen
4 bedroom
5 bath
6 loft
7 storage
8 porch
9 deck

main floor plan
0 1 2   4

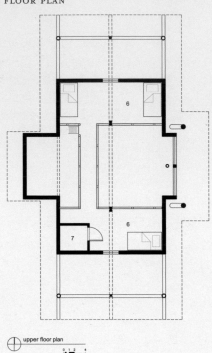

upper floor plan
0 1 2   4

SITE PLAN

SECTIONS

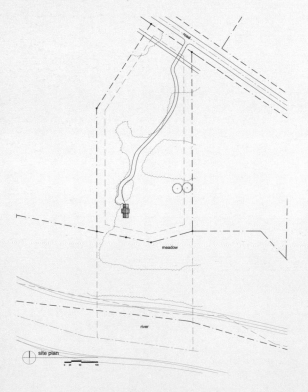

Road

meadow

river

site plan

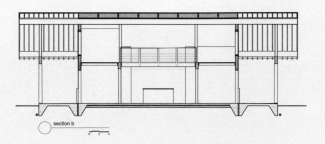

section a
0 2 4

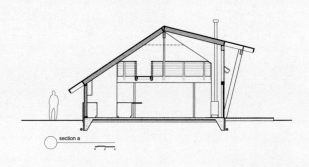

section b
0 2 4

ELEVATIONS

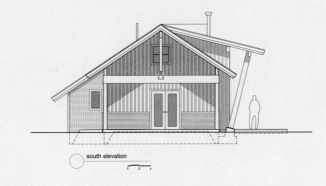

south elevation

west elevation

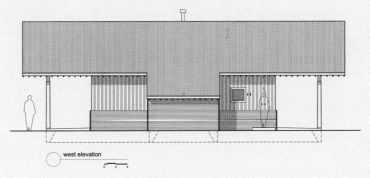

north elevation

east elevation

LEFT AND RIGHT: *A large window wall opens onto a protected deck. The exterior consists of rough-sawn select knotty cedar board-and-batten siding.*

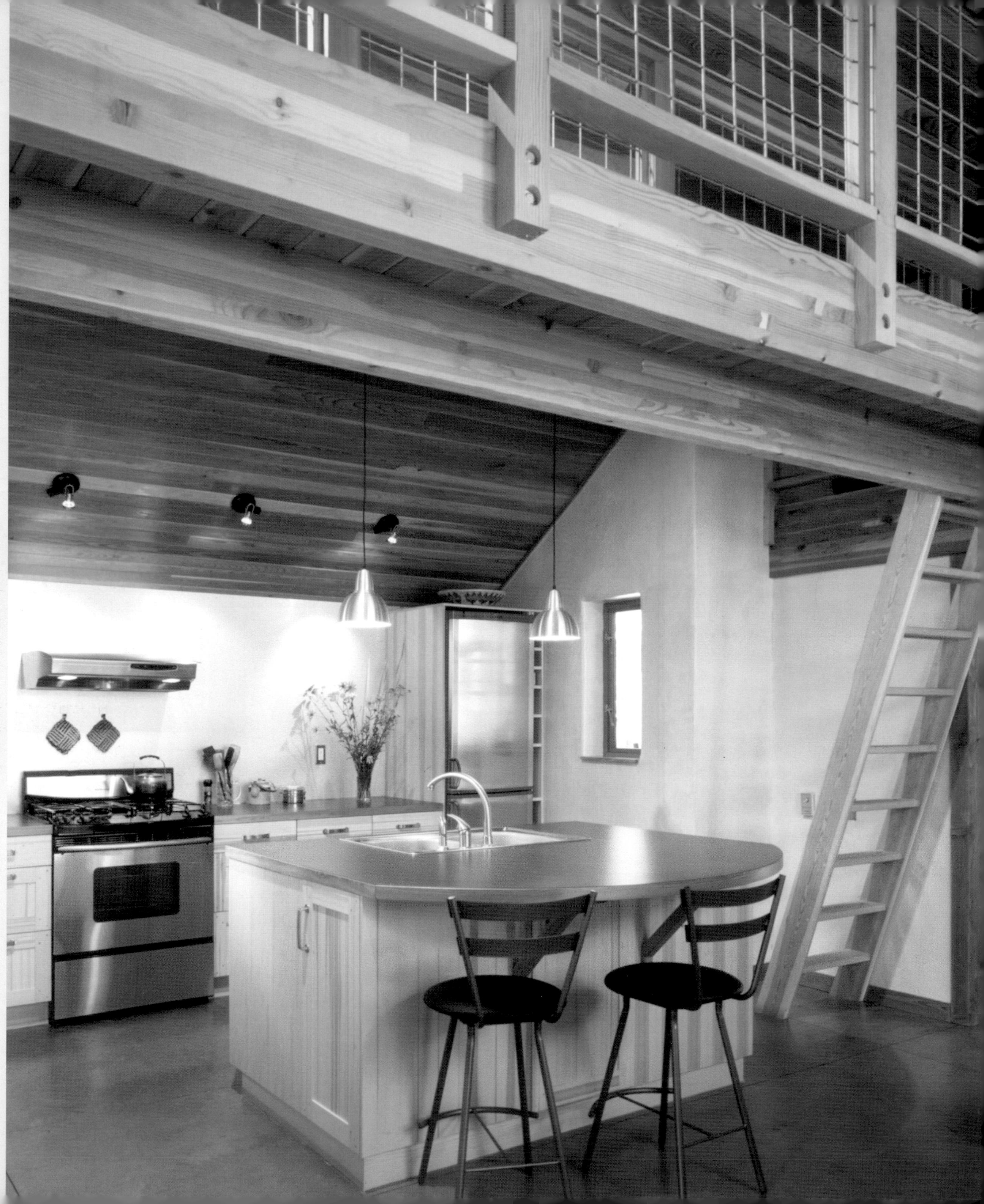

LEFT: *The master bedroom is tucked under the sleeping loft adjacent to the living area.*

RIGHT: *The simple, straightforward design of the house carries through to the single bathroom located on the first floor.*

FOLLOWING PAGES: *The steep metal roof protects the house during the heavy snowfalls in this region.*

GOLOB-FREEMAN
CABIN

ARCHITECT DAVID SALMELA

LOCATION MADELINE ISLAND, WISCONSIN

This small yet dramatic cabin is located on Madeline Island in Lake Superior. It consists of two buildings. The main cabin has a bedroom and a bath and a combined living, dining, and kitchen area. A patio separates this cabin from a small guest cabin with a bedroom and bath. Extending from the patio is a walkway that leads to a dramatic, monolithic white outdoor fireplace that serves as a marker for the site. The cabin itself has been painted black and the ends dark blue, and at times it is almost invisible. The walls of the cabin extend beyond the building, protecting it from the winds. In back of the main cabin is a large screened porch with a butterfly roof.

The stark exterior of the cabin is in strong contrast to the intense color of the interior, where the brightly painted floors and ceiling are red and yellow, respectively. Ribbons of windows run the length of the rectangular structure and embrace the wooded site and views of the lake below.

PHOTOGRAPHER PETER BASTIANELLI-KERZE

FLOOR PLAN

PREVIOUS PAGES: *Views of the long, low cabin and guest house from the front and back of the buildings* RIGHT: *The outdoor fireplace serves as a monolithic marker for the site.*

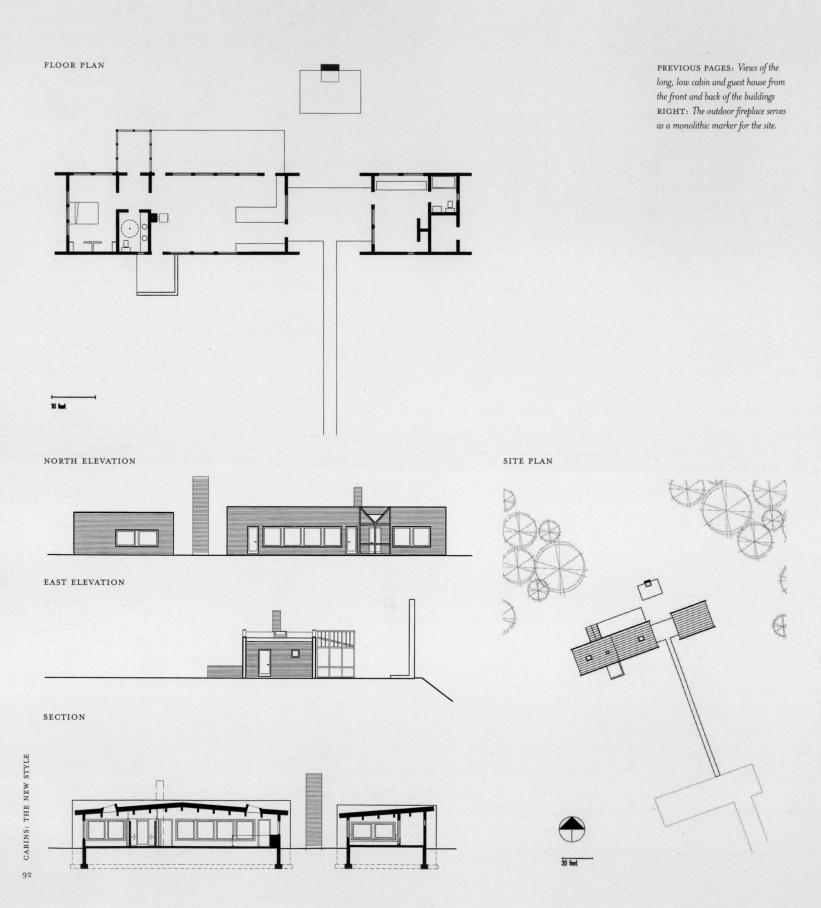

10 feet

NORTH ELEVATION

SITE PLAN

EAST ELEVATION

SECTION

20 feet

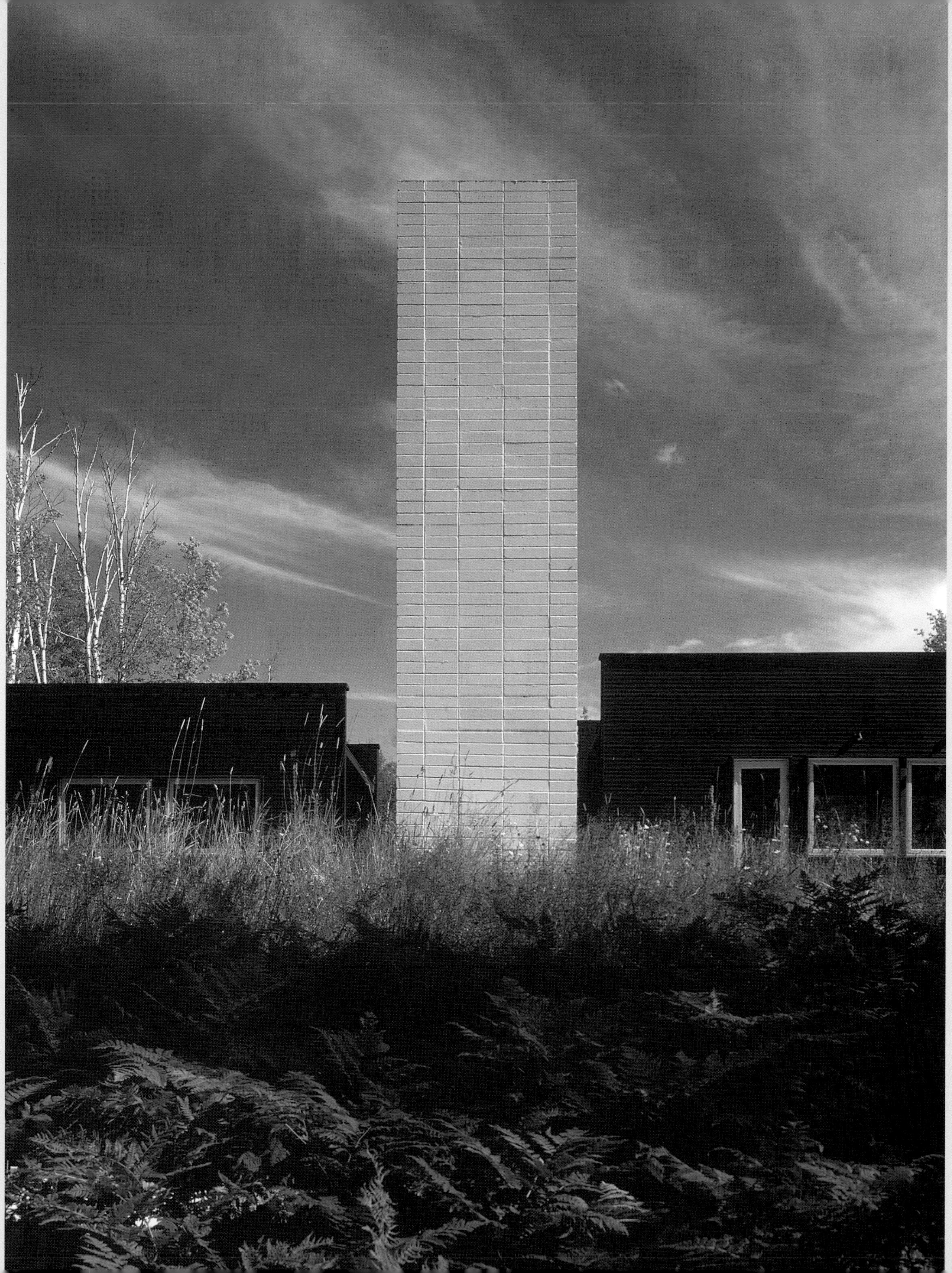

ABOVE: *A view of the main cabin with the porch at the rear*

RIGHT: *A view from the porch toward the outdoor fireplace and guest cabin.*

GOLOB-FREEMAN CABIN

95

LEFT AND ABOVE: *Ample light and bright colors are in stark contrast to the dark exterior.*
FOLLOWING PAGES: *A view from the guest cabin to the main cabin*

CARSON
CABIN

ARCHITECT WILL VAN CAMPEN

LOCATION MONTANA

This 1,700-square-foot dwelling is located on the western bank of the Missouri River overlooking the town of Townsend, Montana. Adjoining the property are the Crimson Bluffs, distinctive, red-colored cliffs whose historical significance derives from their description by Lewis and Clark on their expedition in 1805.

The owner—a California resident, native Montanan, and avid outdoorsman—wanted an economical and low-maintenance retreat for himself and frequent guests. The house was conceived as a reinterpretation of a traditional hunting lodge.

The main floor is organized around a large central room containing living, dining, and kitchen areas. It is oriented toward the panoramic view to the east. This room is flanked by master and guest bedrooms at either end. Each bedroom has its own private porch. A generous deck for socializing extends the entire length of the house. The service spaces—mudroom, bathrooms, and closets—are arranged along the opposite, entry side. A partial basement is accessed from the mudroom and contains mechanical equipment, general storage, and a wine cellar.

PHOTOGRAPHER J. K. LAWRENCE

FLOOR PLAN

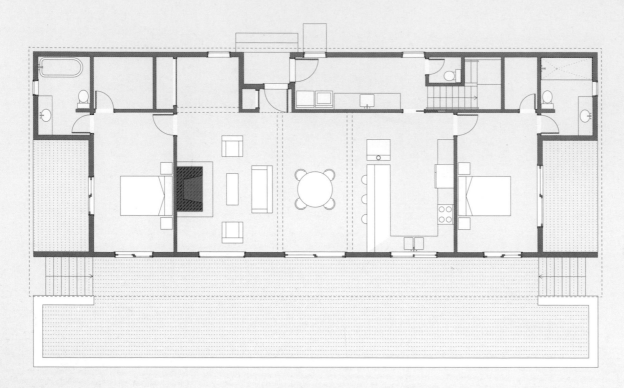

SECTION

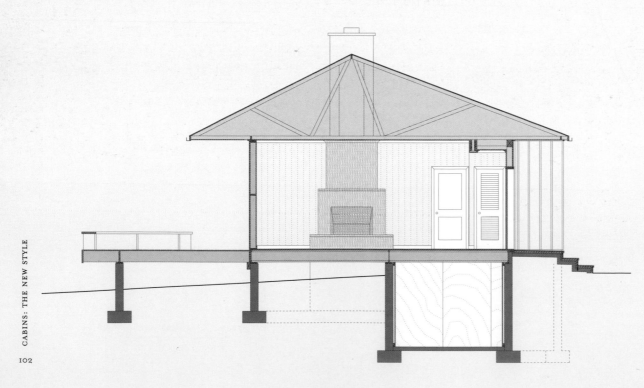

PREVIOUS PAGES: *The rough-cut board-and-batten exterior siding is western red cedar on the house and lodgepole pine on the barn. All exterior and interior wood finishes were custom-sawn at local mills. The roofing is standing-seam steel.*

ABOVE: *Crimson Bluffs was acquired by the federal government and designated a historical landmark in 2003.*

ABOVE: *View upriver from above the Crimson Bluffs*

RIGHT: *The barn at left contains a three-stall garage, workshop, and loft above.*

ABOVE: *View looking west*
LEFT: *A view of the entry; The dogtrot marks the center of the facade.*
RIGHT: *The slightly asymmetrical roof as viewed from the south elevation*
FOLLOWING PAGES: *In the living room, the fireplace is faced with a locally quarried stone called iron slate ledge.*

LEFT AND TOP: *The interior walls and ceiling are ponderosa pine, and the floors are Montana fir plank. The kitchen is open to the living room, and incorporates an antique woodstove for auxiliary heating.*
ABOVE: *The north bedroom and porch with bifurcated views up- and downriver*

FOLLOWING PAGES: *A view from the deck looking north; the continuous bench functions as both a guardrail and seating.*

EVANS
RESIDENCE

ARCHITECT TURNBULL GRIFFIN & HAESLOOP
LOCATION NORTHERN CALIFORNIA

The narrow site for this weekend dwelling overlooks the Pacific Ocean in the resort community of the Sea Ranch in northern California. Rather than building the home on one of the lots nearest the ocean, the architects decided to create three separate structures near the back of the property, where they look diagonally across their own lot out to the ocean, with the meadow landscape flowing through the center of the site. A mature stand of cypress trees marks the edge of the lot.

 The two main buildings, the living/dining/kitchen structure and the master bedroom structure, form two parallel walls, which frame the view out to the Pacific. On the living room side, elements respond to the existing cypress trees, with the dining room bay opening up in a long, horizontal sweep to the bluff and ocean beyond. A wall provides privacy for the master bedroom but allows a filtered view through the cypress out to the ocean. The studio at the rear of the lot overlooks the small compound.

PHOTOGRAPHER JIM ALINDER

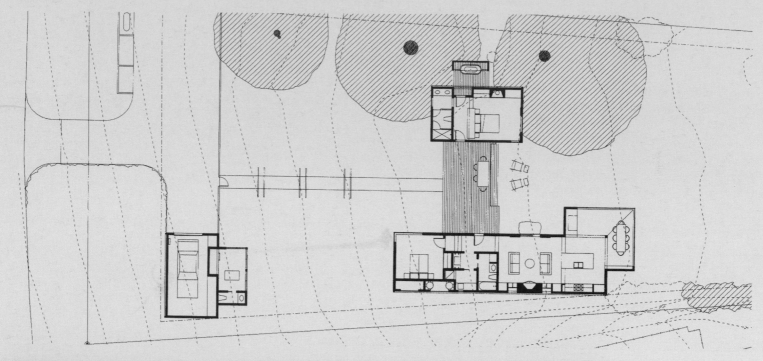

PREVIOUS PAGES AND LEFT:
The large window wall in the living room overlooks cypress trees, while the bay window of the dining room provides views across the meadow to the ocean.

LEFT: *The master bedroom structure and the living/dining/kitchen structure are parallel to each other.*

ABOVE: *A view from the living area to the cypress trees*
RIGHT: *The kitchen and dining area have a view through the bay window to the ocean.*

LEFT: *The open kitchen as seen from the dining area*
RIGHT: *The living room fireplace*

ABOVE LEFT AND ABOVE:
The master bedroom and bathroom

ABOVE: *The studio as seen from the main living structures*
RIGHT: *Interior view of the studio*
FOLLOWING PAGES: *The compound as seen from the bluff*

MEADOW CABIN

ARCHITECT BALANCE ASSOCIATES ARCHITECTS

LOCATION WASHINGTON

This 1,600-square-foot cabin is nestled into a small grove of trees in the middle of a large river valley in eastern Washington. The cabin is oriented to capture landscape and mountain views while blocking unwanted views of adjacent homes. The living and dining rooms are in a two-story space surrounded with windows and open onto patios on three sides. In the more enclosed area at the rear of the house are the kitchen, master bedroom and bathroom, and utility spaces. Upstairs is a loft and screened sleeping porch. A small, detached carport and storage area are located nearby.

Both the cabin and the garage take shape as unadorned shed forms relating to the vernacular farm structures in the area. The exterior building materials have been kept simple. The siding is rough-sawn cedar channel siding, and the roofs are standing-seam galvanized steel. Large overhangs with log columns create entry porches and patios to provide protection from both the winter snow and the summer heat.

PHOTOGRAPHER STEVE KEATING

UPPER FLOOR PLAN

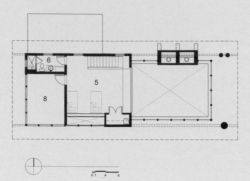

PREVIOUS PAGES: *The extensively glazed two-story volume of the house contains the living and dining areas.*

MAIN FLOOR PLAN

1 entry
2 living
3 dining
4 kitchen
5 loft
6 bath
7 utility
8 screened porch
9 master bedroom
10 master bath

SITE PLAN

SKETCH

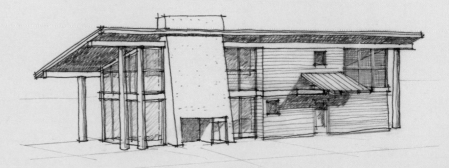

ELEVATIONS

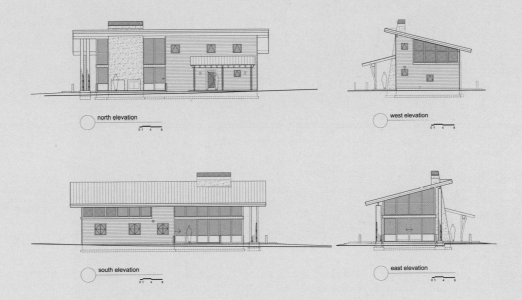

north elevation   0 1   4   8

west elevation   0 1   4   8

south elevation   0 1   4   8

east elevation   0 1   4   8

SECTIONS

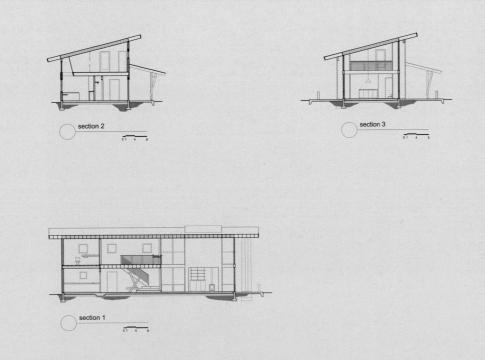

section 2   0 1   4   8

section 3   0 1   4   8

section 1   0 1   4   8

LEFT: *A screened sleeping porch wraps around the second level.*
BELOW LEFT, AND RIGHT: *The shed roof design recalls the design of many of the farm buildings in this rural area.*

LEFT AND ABOVE: *The ceiling of the two-story living and dining area is 1-by-4-inch mixed-grain Douglas fir.*

LEFT AND ABOVE: *Large sliding glass doors open the living and dining areas onto one of three patios, one of which has an outdoor fireplace.*

LEFT: *The kitchen is located at the rear of the cabin under the sleeping loft.*

RIGHT: *A view from the entry of the stairs to the loft and the living area beyond*

FOLLOWING PAGES: *A view of the east elevation with the carport and storage shed to the right.*

MATTHEW CABIN

ARCHITECT DAVID SALMELA

LOCATION GULL LAKE, MINNESOTA

The location of this cabin was the key to its success. It replaced the client's existing cabin, which had burned to the ground in a fire. The old cabin sat parallel to this north-facing lot on a gentle point extending into the lake, thus dividing the lot into lakeside and roadside. The new 20-by-56-foot, two-story house was placed perpendicular to the water, creating outdoor rooms to the east and west for sunrises and sunsets as well as enhancing lake views from both sides.

     The interior walls of the cabin, as well as a separate sauna and garage, are sheathed with cypress on the ceilings. The first floor is slate and contains the living, dining, kitchen, and study areas. An open stair leads to the second floor, where a hallway that leads to the three bedrooms and two bathrooms is open to the living area below. One end of the hallway leads to a screened porch while the other end becomes a small library area. The outdoor rooms that flank the east and west sides of the house are framed with white stained wood, screened with 2-by-2-inch slats.

     The house, sauna, and garage appear to float on a field of native grasses conveying a pastoral scene one expects from a Minnesota cabin.

PHOTOGRAPHER PETER BASTIANELLI-KERZE

ELEVATIONS

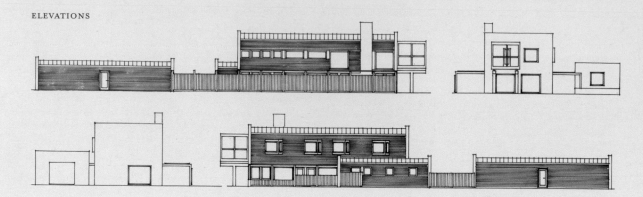

PREVIOUS PAGES: *Slanted windows at the second level provide views of the lake.*
RIGHT: *An outdoor room separates the main house from the sauna.*
BELOW RIGHT: *A view of the outdoor room with the sauna beyond*

FIRST FLOOR PLAN/SITE PLAN

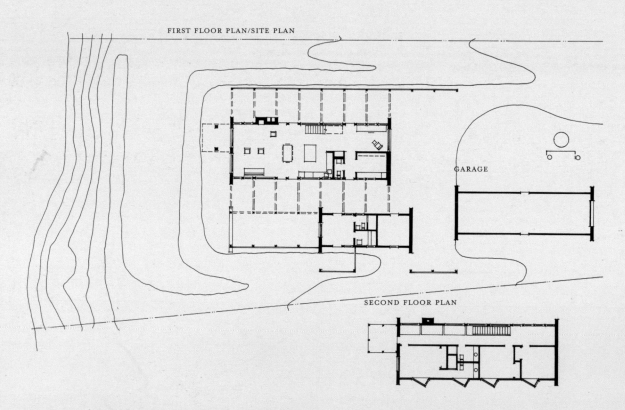

GARAGE

SECOND FLOOR PLAN

ABOVE: *The kitchen is to the right of an open stairway that leads to the second floor bedrooms.*
LEFT: *The stairway is screened with 2-by-2-inch painted wooden slats.*
RIGHT: *A view of the open living, dining, and kitchen areas; the ceiling is covered with cyprus planks.*

LEFT: *The living area opens onto an outdoor room.*

ABOVE: *The first floor study has Slate floors that are used throughout the downstairs level.*

LEFT AND RIGHT: *A corridor runs the length of the second floor and opens to the living area below on one side and to the bedrooms on the other. There is a library nook on one end and a porch on the other.*
FOLLOWING PAGES: *A view of the cabin as seen from the lake with the outdoor rooms flanking either side and the secondfloor porch cantilevered above*

WINTERGREEN CABIN

ARCHITECT BALANCE ASSOCIATES ARCHITECTS

LOCATION WASHINGTON

This 1,600-square-foot cabin in the Methow Valley in the Pacific Northwest is built into a steep hillside overlooking a stream and offers views of the mountains in the distance. A concrete base containing the garage and utility spaces anchors the cabin.

Upstairs the living and dining areas and kitchen are contained within a glass box that opens onto suspended decks. Large roof overhangs protect the glass wall from the elements and direct sunlight in the summer.

At the rear of the cabin and nestled into the hillside are the bedrooms and bathrooms. They also have smaller windows and lower ceiling heights. Dividing the public and private spaces is an area that contains the entry, stairs to the garage, and a small office. A large, continuous shed roof of corrugated steel gathers the three spaces into one form. The exterior is sheathed in rough-sawn knotty cedar siding. The decks are made from Trex, which is composed of recycled materials.

PHOTOGRAPHER STEVE KEATING

LOWER FLOOR PLAN

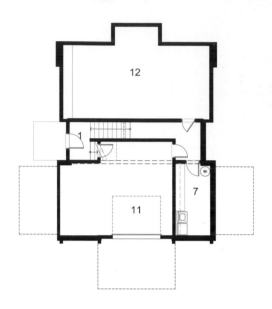

MAIN FLOOR PLAN

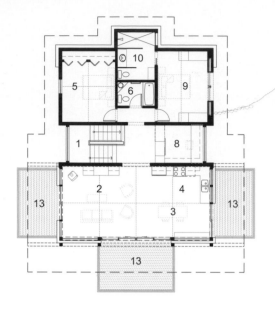

PREVIOUS PAGES: *The structural frame of the main living area is pulled to the exterior of the glass wall, allowing the walls to be primarily glass.*

1 entry
2 living
3 dining
4 kitchen
5 guest bedroom
6 bath
7 utility
8 office
9 master bedroom
10 master bath
11 garage
12 storage
13 deck

SITE PLAN

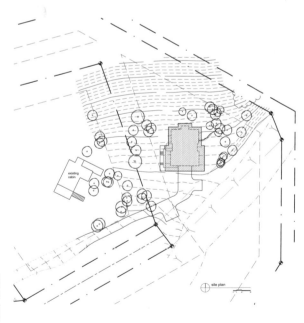

SECTION

EAST ELEVATION

east elevation

NORTH ELEVATION

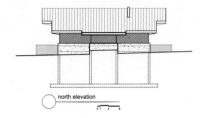

north elevation

WEST ELEVATION

west elevation

SOUTH ELEVATION

south elevation

SECTION 1

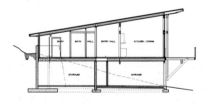

SECTION 2

SECTION 3

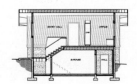

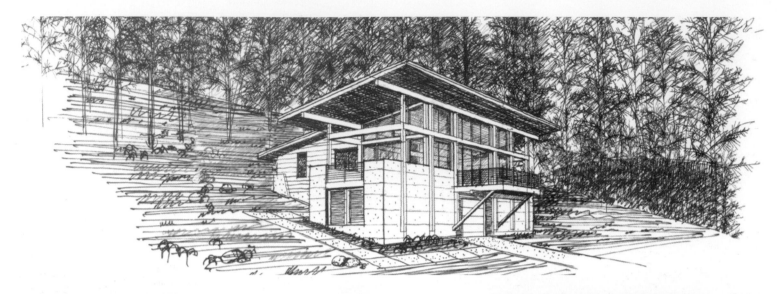

LEFT: *The main entry to the cabin separates the living area from the bedrooms.*

ABOVE: *The cabin rests on a concrete block foundation with a garage access.*

RIGHT: *The living area enjoys views of the distant mountains.*

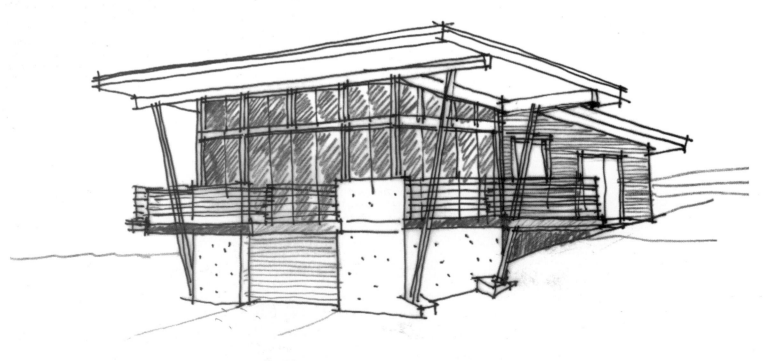

FAR LEFT AND LEFT: *Details of the deck supports*
RIGHT: *The entry is marked by horizontal corrugated steel.*

LEFT: *The main living area has high ceilings made of knotty cedar.* RIGHT: *View of the living area and stairs to the garage from the entry*

VINEYARD CABIN

ARCHITECT MOSKOW ARCHITECTS

LOCATION MASSACHUSETTS

This 2,700-square-foot three-bedroom dwelling is located on a six-acre lot in a thick scrub oak forest on Martha's Vineyard in Massachusetts. Constructed of Douglas fir with white cedar shingles, the project consists of two buildings, one for sleeping and the other containing the living, dining, and kitchen areas. An outdoor courtyard was created between the two buildings. An entry allée brings visitors from the parking area to the buildings. An outdoor shower is located along the allée for a quick rinse after coming from the beach and before entering the house.

An independent umbrella roof supported by columns creates a protective enclosure for the living spaces. A porch runs the length of both buildings to protect the rooms from summer heat. Living and sleeping areas remain cool without mechanical systems.

PHOTOGRAPHER ERIC ROTH

FIRST FLOOR PLAN

PREVIOUS PAGES: *The cabin consists of two buildings, one for bedrooms on the left and one for the living, dining, and kitchen areas on the right.*

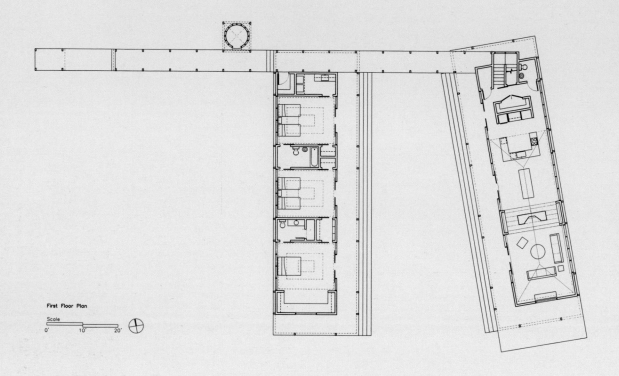

First Floor Plan

Scale

0'   10'   20'

SLEEPING WING SECTIONS

LIVING WING SECTIONS

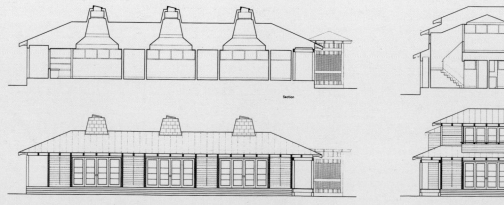

Section

Section

ABOVE: *A long wooden allée runs from the parking area, past an outdoor shower, to the two buildings.*
RIGHT: *A view of the living area at night*

LEFT: *Deep porches surround the buildings to provide shelter from the summer heat.*
ABOVE: *A view down the allée from the parking area*
ABOVE RIGHT: *The outdoor shower*

ABOVE: *Living area with the dining and kitchen areas beyond.*
RIGHT: *Each bedroom has a large skylight.*
FAR RIGHT: *The dining area is on the other side of the fireplace.*

RIGHT: *The roofs are lead-coated copper and are structurally independent from the buildings beneath.*

CANYON CABIN

ARCHITECT BALANCE ASSOCIATES ARCHITECTS

LOCATION WASHINGTON

The project sits in a deep, narrow valley in the foothills of the Cascade Mountains. The site has been ranched and mined since the early pioneer days. In order to reduce the scale of the 3,000-square-foot dwelling, it was divided into three separate buildings: the main cabin, a garage, and a bunkhouse. A large shed roof unites the three buildings. The connection between the cabin and the house is enclosed, providing a mudroom hallway adjacent to the utility room. A covered breezeway joins the cabin and the bunkhouse. The compound is arranged in a U-shaped pattern, creating a southern-facing central courtyard.

The extraordinary beauty of this natural setting led to a design that visually unites the interior with the exterior. For example, exterior building materials continue indoors. Large glass walls on each end of the main living space allow the views of the spectacular valley walls that rise 3,500 feet off the valley floor. The glass walls protrude in a U shape at the north end to create more interior space connected to this primary view. On the south end, the glass wall recedes to allow for a larger southern patio. The roof overhangs on both ends were calculated so as to not block the view of the mountain peaks while controlling seasonal solar exposure on the southern end. Weathering steel was used for roofs and upper wall siding, and river rock walls form the base of the main building and extend out into the landscape to provide retaining walls for patios and courtyards.

PHOTOGRAPHER STEVE KEATING

MAIN FLOOR PLAN

PREVIOUS PAGES: *The main structure consists of log beams and columns. The log structure is exposed both inside and out.*

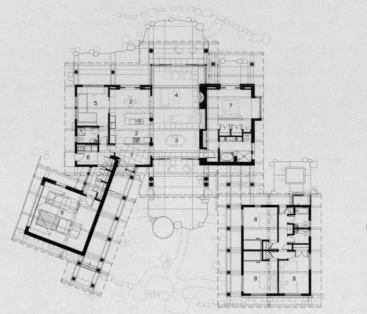

1   entry
2   kitchen
3   dining
4   living
5   study
6   utility room
7   master suite
8   bedroom
9   garage

SITE PLAN

CONCEPT SKETCHES

site plan

SOUTH ELEVATION

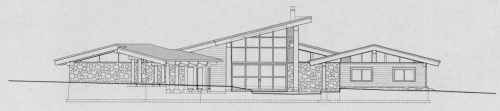

EAST ELEVATION

NORTH ELEVATION

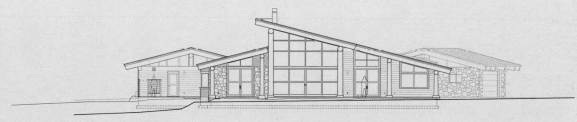

WEST ELEVATION

LEFT, BELOW LEFT, AND
RIGHT: *The design of the cabin
incorporates walls of glass to take
advantage of the spectacular scenery.
To reduce the mass of the 3,000-
square-foot plan, the compound
consists of three separate buildings
under one roof.*

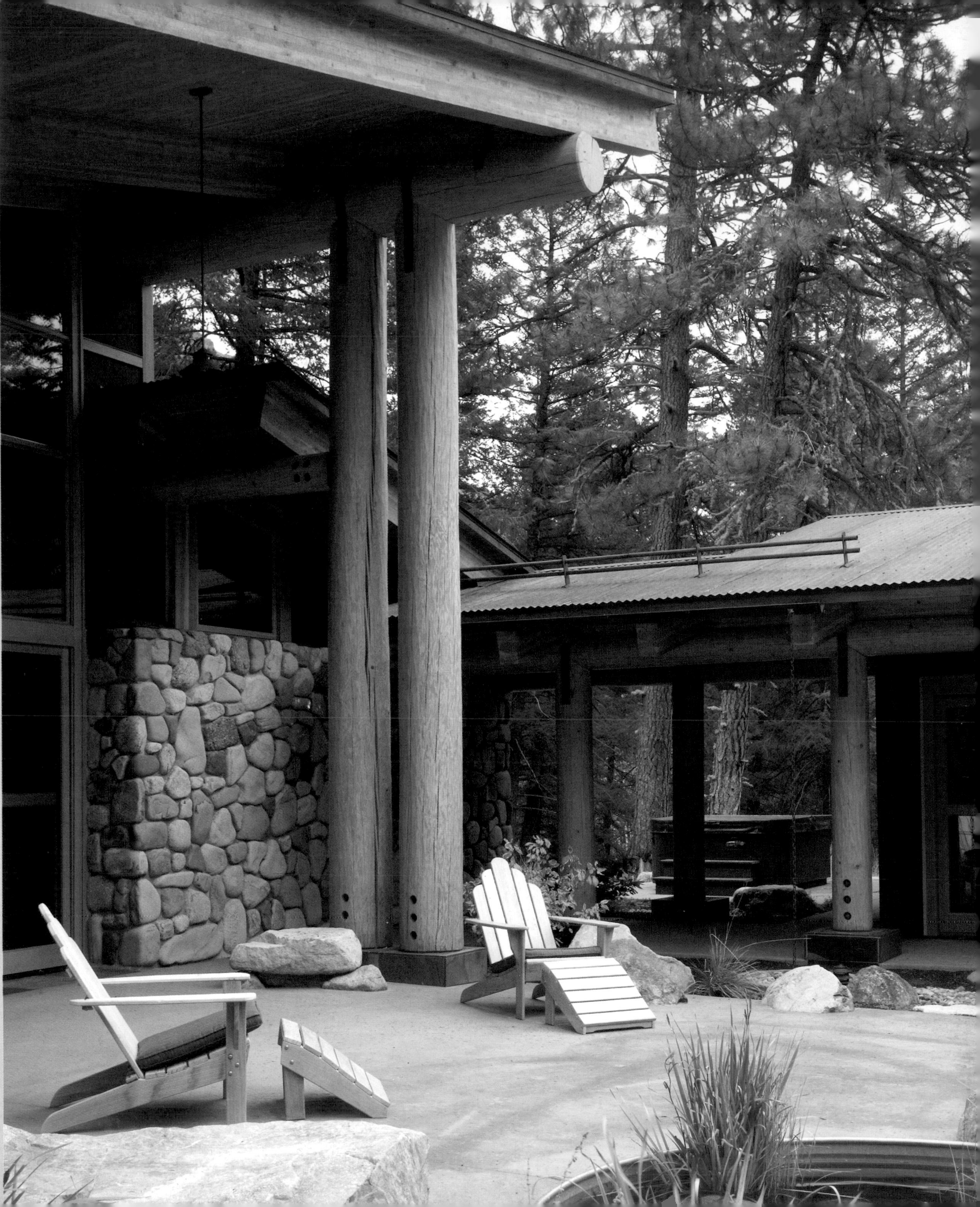

LEFT: *A breezeway connects the*
main cabin to the bunkhouse.
ABOVE: *A view of the garage*

LEFT: *The fireplace in the living area is constructed of river stone.*
ABOVE: *A view of the study in the main cabin*
ABOVE RIGHT: *The master bedroom*
FOLLOWING PAGES: *A view of the main house and bunkhouse*